OH CONSCIENCE

WILLIAM KOCH JR.

OH CONSCIENCE

TATE PUBLISHING
AND ENTERPRISES, LLC

Published by Tate Publishing & Enterprises, LLC
127 E. Trade Center Terrace | Mustang, Oklahoma 73064 USA
1.888.361.9473 | www.tatepublishing.com

Tate Publishing is committed to excellence in the publishing industry. The company reflects the philosophy established by the founders, based on Psalm 68:11,
"The Lord gave the word and great was the company of those who published it."

Book design copyright © 2015 by Tate Publishing, LLC. All rights reserved.
Cover design by Bill Francis Peralta
Interior design by Gram Telen

Published in the United States of America

ISBN: 978-1-68118-154-7
Poetry / General
15.07.03

The Rock

Locked against the tide
Rock firm atop a ledge
Wave's crash and retreat
Still rock holds the pledge
Battered and worn down
Ageless and always strong
Survives storms of hurting
Fighting through the wrong
Day and nighttime sentry
With good and the bad
Calmed assurance mostly
Also knowing of the sad
Breaking past the sorrow
Struggling with the pain
Rock stays brave forever
Under weight of strain
Turmoil is everywhere
Rock stands steely fast
Dreams washed away
Rock will always last
Pledged to hold firmly
Evermore on the clock
Waves of tides crash
My son Bill, the rock

(6-4-2012)

Locked against the tide
Rock firm atop a ledge
Wave's crash and retreat
Still rock holds the pledge
Battered and worn down
Ageless and always strong
Survives storms of hurting
Fighting through the wrong
Day and nighttime sentry
With good and the bad
Calmed assurance mostly
Also knowing of the sad
Breaking past the sorrow
Struggling with the pain
Rock stays brave forever
Under weight of strain
Turmoil is everywhere
Rock stands steely fast
Dreams washed away
Rock will always last
Pledged to hold firmly
Evermore on the clock
Waves of tides crash
My son Bill, the rock

The
Rock

A Mother's Life Cycle

Searching	Interested	Attracted	Excitement	Touching	Kissing

Searching   Together
Talking   Lust
Walking   Bonding
Hugging   Love
Lost   Sex
Sorrow   Caring
Broken   Sharing
Courage   Hurting
Emptiness   Adorned
Hunger   Protect
Helpless   Cherish
Longing   Respond
Worship   Love
Tribute   Desire
Pray   Coupled
Honor   Create
Acclaim   Endure
Strong   Labor
Sob   Pain
Angered   Crying
Hurt   Birth
Sickened   Elation
Weakened   Love
Weep   Caress
Pain   Nurture
Horrified   Shelter
React   Defend
Worry   Teach
Distressed   Raise
Treasured   Reason
Humbled   Suffer
Transport   Discipline
Miss   Provide
                 Pride

Traveled	Agonize	Release	Admire	Congratulate	Respect

Release the Poems

Walking slowly by a wrought iron gate
Noticing something amiss that I can relate
Standing before a mansion of lonely grey stone
My demeanor turned fast to a lower tone
Seeing alphabets scattered on the ground
Knowing full well, a clue was now found
Where did these words run to now hide
Escaping incomplete, for a sentence inside

The home of an author who has had his way
Convincing the words that night to then stay
He teases them with respect and proper use
Or terrifies them with eternal verbiage abuse
Linking these words to form a type of story
One of true love, mystery or of a greater glory
Spending hours and hours ready at type set
Controlled by the writer as his teacher's pet

Oh how special he writes at his most noble craft
Criticize it or him, you beg quickly for his wrath
The smart artist of wordage, to complete a score
Interest to the reader, freedom from the daily bore
Author remains real as he has a true heart
Penning an ending to every book he does start
Making sense of timelines and a real life plot
Long or short, accounts that always tell a lot

Not like the poet, a writer so shallow and frail
He links rhymes together that miserably fail
Misuses words and comma's for his own short gain
Always a sap, referring to tears as the falling rain
Not very good at proper English or point of view
Matter of fact, his work, selfish as we already knew
People don't understand or see the poetry content
Much less, do they even get, the versifier's intent

So for all his brawny boasts and fancy avowals
Consonants flee along with the skittish vowels
People listen and take heed, lock up your homes
Words run amok, when poets, release the poems

(12-21-2011)

Contents

Foreword

Oh Conscience—as in my first book from Tate Publishing, *Casualties of War*—reveals deep emotions of pride, sorrow, tribute, and of loss by individuals in a family, left in a wake of remorse, loneness and heartache. The loss of one young family member, Cpl. Steven R. Koch, KIA in Afghanistan on March 3, 2008, was and is too much to bear, followed by a second of Lynne C. Koch, May 6, 2010, of PTSD becomes insufferable at times. The agony and sorrow easily results in a loss of family and friends, relationship connections, concentration of daily routines along with focus on time or details in general.

The continual release of words and images from my deepest thoughts and raging rants of life cover the extremes of feelings and passion. With the second book through Tate, *Patriotic Passion*, I tried to release more of the dedication to heroic and courageous men and women who serve our nation along with my family's dealings with the daily and at times hour-to-hour struggle to continue on in existence. I use the word existence as it fits better the plight most of the time instead of life or living. Those of us with such losses all walk the crowded path of anguish, yet must still travel it alone and in our own spiritual essence. This collection of fifty plus poems, verses, and tributes are just a small amount of the over four hundred written, imaged, now in print and those that wait in the wings or have been posted on Facebook. *Oh Conscience*'s poetic words and graphic images will lead you to reflect and realize the compassion; feel the loss and pride by a family filled with emotions for their loved ones. The words may also educate in a small way of the sacrifice made by a man or woman, soldier or sailor, marine or airmen, which gave of themselves to protect all of us, defend America and her freedoms. There is power in words and images that can reveal your own self-awareness and give you the insight to what these brave service people and their families sacrificed and continue to give. Even when they have left the service, been wounded, and suffered the loss of the ultimate sacrifice of a loved one, they still serve.

> Don't question where courage comes from, be
> hopeful it never runs out.

—William Koch Jr.

Fury

FURY

fu·rynoun \ˈfyu̇r-ē\
: violent anger
: wild and dangerous force
: Plural *furies*

Full Definition of Fury

1. intense, disordered, and often destructive rage

2. a: capitalized: any of the avenging deities in Greek mythology who torment criminals and inflict plagues
   b: an avenging spirit
   c: one who resembles an avenging spirit; especially: a spiteful woman

3. extreme fierceness or violence

4. a state of inspired exaltation

Examples of Fury

- I could see the *fury* in her eyes.
- Nothing could contain his *fury* over their accusations.
- He turned away from them in *fury*.

- The hurricane unleashed its *fury* on hundreds of homes and businesses.

Origin of Fury

Middle English furie, from Latin furia, from furere to rage
First Known Use: 14th century

Related to Fury

Synonyms
battle-ax (or battle-axe), dragon lady, shrew, harpy, harridan, termagant, virago, vixen

Another Lot

Alone, in a chair
No one to the left
The right also bare

Distant voices play
Aloof to a tribute
The price they pay

Anthem of liberty
Sung in splendor
Eyes cannot see

A nation has forgot
Of the self sacrifice
Left to another lot

Alone, at the front
Soldier at arms
Boots of the grunt

Families give to thee
Fought with blood
Freedom isn't free

Day to day stress
For the unknown
In a turmoil mess

Serving with pride
Tributes earned
No place to hide

Does anyone care
Left or the right
Alone, in a chair

(7-11-2012)

The Crossed Line

I let emotion
Take me on a wild ride
Of agony's toll
That refuses to hide
It taunts so
With relentless zeal
Not caring much
Of what others feel
In silent expression
Through written word
From restless dreams
I'm sure I heard
Toward one goal
There's no way to win
Yet still alone
Through thick or thin
In living hope
Of light to shine
Past the dark
Before the crossed line
Time is age
Not to be left behind
Memories dwell
For a pathway to find
Ink to paper

Lend a tool to forms
Of prideful images
In pressed uniforms
Pen that flows
Passion expressed
Past the trauma
Of the distressed
Feel the hold
As sorrow writes
Through years
Day or over nights
I let emotion
Take me on a wild ride
Of agony's toll
I refused to hide

(5-29-2014)

THE CROSSED LINE

I let emotion
Take me on a wild ride
Of agony's toll
That refuses to hide
It taunts so
With relentless zeal
Not caring much
Of what others feel
In silent expression
Through written word
From restless dreams
I'm sure I heard
Toward one goal
There's no way to win
Yet still alone
Through thick or thin
In living hope
Of light to shine
Past the dark
Before the crossed line

Time is age
Not to be left behind
Memories dwell
For a pathway to find
Ink to paper
Lend a tool to forms
Of prideful images
In pressed uniforms
Pen that flows
Passion expressed
Past the trauma
Of the distressed
Feel the hold
As sorrow writes
Through years
Day or over nights
I let emotion
Take me on a wild ride
Of agony's toll
I refused to hide

Wm Koch Jr. 5-29-2014©

The Finish Line

The track of life like the oval of race
Running for your life in hopes to place
Win or lose it comes with a rough road
Colors, a number and saddled with a load

There are cloudy days with lots of rain
Smooth galloping but tight turns of pain
Sun baked course to harden a timely path
Winning brings roses, the thorns the wrath

Moments run fast yet lags the finish line
For the race to the final is never define
Taking on the journey and its rough ride
Dashing at full speed on a forever glide

Jockey for position, breaking the gate
Speeding forward, with blinders too late
Looking back, yet forward, fast ahead
Endless race shall be, a forever dread

First to third than back to the rear
Front running is short lived with a tear
Around each bend you lose distance fast
Struggle to regroup to not draw the last

As years are laps of this darken track
Passing others there is no looking back
Odds stacked, bets went heavy to light
The finish line is lost, lost into the night

(7-25-2013)

The track of life like the oval of race
Running for your life in hopes to place
Win or lose it comes with a rough road
Colors, a number and saddled with a load

There are cloudy days with lots of rain
Smooth galloping but tight turns of pain
Sun baked course to harden a timely path
Winning brings roses, the thorns the wrath

Moments run fast yet lags the finish line
For the race to the final is never define
Taking on the journey and its rough ride
Dashing at full speed on a forever glide

Jockey for position, breaking the gate
Speeding forward, with blinders too late
Looking back, get forward, fast ahead
Endless race shall be, a forever dread

First to third than back to the rear
Front running is short lived with a tear
Around each bend you lose distance fast
Struggle to regroup to not draw the last

As years are laps of this darken track
Passing others there is no looking back
Odds stacked, bets went heavy to light
The finish line is lost, lost into the night

The Finish Line

Wr Roch Jr.   7-25-2013©

Caged Tiger

The caged tiger paces
Back and forth eternally
Dulling his keen senses
Master wants this to be
Wearing down his will
Made to jump through a ring
Thinking he's really tamed
Left without much sting
Alas, the tiger waits his turn
The leash will soon fall away
The lock will also be picked
The tiger will rule the day
Remember not to taunt or tease
Neither to whip with a snap
The tiger's teeth are sharp
First he'll eat, then a nap
Doesn't look to tame others
Though sometimes, he is a beast
Just looking for some respect
Not the most, just not the least
Guards his family to the death
Loyalty of heart is a must
Walking the weary walk
Standing yet, in settling dust
Master, take this warning

Imprisoned don't forget faces
Back and forth eternally
The caged tiger paces

(8-3-2012)

Cold Frosty Brew

Sitting and relaxing with a cold frosty brew
Checking in, with the normal Chili's crew
Ponder in thought, whether to write a poem
Thinking now, I'll just head for my home
To stare at walls, that always stares back
To type out a few PC lines, of poetry hack

With no real direction and no known drive
Those few lines of verse, keep me alive
Through the night, more words I shall add
A few more letters, to turn it agony sad
With a final stanza to make others content
Not all my writings are on a sorrow bent

When all I really want, what I want to do
Go back in time of years, just for a few
When my life had hopes and true reason
Now it's always the dark mourning season
You know, I think, I'll just have another one
Think of a loving daughter and a brave son

Be quiet and respectful to what people think
Though no one bothers past their next drink
Even the anthem on a TV gets no respect

Many only care about themselves, I detect
So will this tribute prose, even make a dent
Reaching to others is my only true intent

Food for thought, feelings they really are
Or are my written words, just a bit too far
You know, I think, I'll just have another one
Think of a loving daughter and a brave son
Check in some more with the Chili's crew
Sitting and staring into a cold frosty brew

(10-21-2012)

William Koch Jr.

Eyes of Plenty

Don't mind me now, I'm all alone
Standing firm in spirit and tone
Stayed content through the night
It's harder each hour of daylight

Will my faith hear my lonely call
To rescue me from my eternal fall
I walk every day as nothing is wrong
What most don't know, the walk is long

Long and fearful, that it never ends
A path that follows forever bends
Alone with a crowd along the lane
Eyes of plenty, overlooking the pain

Don't mind me now, I'm all alone
I live and die with each sun shown
Have felt the apathy of the fight
As it's never far from my sight

Will my faith hear my lonely call
A standing message seems too tall
Walk with a soul to calm my fears
Rest along a river of sorrow tears

Long and fearful that it never ends
Life on a journey, refusing the amends
A crowd listens, waits but cannot see
Eyes of plenty; look right through me

(7-25-2013)

Don't mind me now, I'm all alone
Standing firm in spirit and tone
Stayed content through the night
It's harder each hour of daylight
Will my faith hear my lonely call
To rescue me from my eternal fall
I walk every day as nothing is wrong
What most don't know, the walk is long

Long and fearful, that it never ends
A path that follows forever bends
Alone with a crowd along the lone
Eyes of plenty, overlooking the pain
Don't mind me now, I'm all alone
I live and die with each sun shown
Have felt the apathy of the fight
As it's never far from my sight

Will my faith hear my lonely call
A standing message seems too tall
Walk with a soul to calm my fears
Rest along a river of sorrow tears
Long and fearful that it never ends
Life on a journey, refusing the amends
A crowd listens, waits but cannot see
Eyes of plenty, look right through me

Colorless

Shadow black, shadow white
Trace lines left without the fight
Hidden in the thin of thick air
Escaping view of visual despair
Colorless soul with tortured heart
Compassion casualty from depart
vMind of mush with nowhere to go

Shadow dark, shadow light
Framed image of agony's plight
Freedom spirit is the eternal flame
Everything left is never the same
Colorless is the outline to stay
Night blends gray into the day
A vision of the silhouette soul
Visible vision, impossible goal

Shadow daily, shadow night
Struggle against wrong or right
Words of sorrow from a strain
Casting awareness past the pain
Colorless brings no tint, no tone

Blank expression as a cobble stone
Down a path cut for only the few
Colorless image, colorless hue

(12-18-2013)

Colorless

Wm. Koch Jr.   12-18-2013©

Shadow black, shadow white
Trace lines left without the fight
Hidden in the thin of thick air
Escaping view of visual despair
Colorless soul with tortured heart
Compassion casualty from depart
Hollow of body from head to toe
Mind of mush with nowhere to go

Shadow dark, shadow light
Framed image of agony's plight
Freedom spirit is the eternal flame
Everything left is never the same
Colorless is the outline to stay
Night blends gray into the day
A vision of the silhouette soul
Visible vision , impossible goal

Shadow daily, shadow night
Struggle against wrong or right
Words of sorrow from a strain
Casting awareness past the pain
Colorless brings no tint, no tone
Blank expression as a cobble stone
Down a path cut for only the few
Colorless image, colorless hue

In a World

In a world with no interest
I'm sorry, I see it very plain
Dull and hollow of concern
Empty pit that I must refrain

As caring and trust are gone
I see no reason for it at all
It was here before, I remember
Now it doesn't answer my call

Dark and moody with disgust
Angry with intolerance to spare
Feeling trampled over each day
As it seems, it doesn't really care

Let us not forget, there are some
Praying and offer sincere thought
Those few come with a high cost
They too, will soon be caught

Trapped by caring too much
Hard to imagine that this is so
Tears fall without any warning
Once started, a never ending flow

In a world of such great beauty
People just get in the way
Kindness, so rare to now find
I know, not a pleasant thing to say

Alas, empty are my true feelings
I've seen a final heartbreaking kiss
Tragic and sadness overwhelmed
In a world with no interest

(6-8-2012)

In My Stairwell

Out, in my stairwell
Where light shines in
Daydreams happen
Not where I've been

I can catch a smoke
Or a call or two
No worries really
Of what I have to do

Out, in my stairwell
There's air to breath
Calm and relaxed
No issues to seethe

Its quiet and peaceful
Where I shed a tear
Out of weather fronts
Anytime of the year

Out, in my stairwell
Its dark at times too
Nightmares appear
No matter what I do

A place I'm myself
I hold no easy grudge
Alone in tranquility
For there is no judge

Out, in my stairwell
Where light shines in
Daydreams happen
Not where I've been

(6-7-2012)

The Lonely Post

Looking back at the then and the now
Reflected anguish of the when, the how
Of plans and dreams gone far astray
In years forgotten from just yesterday

In each life there is a given plight
Forging through the good living fight
Serving others while making the most
Love with compassion, the lonely post

Air drains from the body and a soul
Bleeds out slow but so out of control
That life, what's left, on a ledger list
Being lost in shadows of sorrow mist

A neighborhood now quiet and so serene
Ignores the agony as the present scene
The lives affected with apathy's glow
Seek recluse while no one will know

The world goes on in its quest of life
Shuns discourse or tragic human strife
Discards any pain of a wandering ghost
The one on a perch, the lonely post

(7-24-2013)

The
Lonely
Post

Wm Koch Jr
7-29-2013©

Looking back at the then and the now
Reflected anguish of the when, the how
Of plans and dreams gone far astray
In years forgotten from just yesterday

In each life there is a given plight
Forging through the good living fight
Serving others while making the most
Love with compassion, the lonely post

Air drains from the body and a soul
Bleeds out slow but so out of control
That life, what's left, on a ledger list
Being lost in shadows of sorrow mist

A neighborhood now quiet and so serene
Ignores the agony as the present scene
The lives affected with apathy's glow
Seek recluse while no one will know

The world goes on in its quest of life
Shuns discourse or tragic human strife
Discards any pain of a wandering ghost
The one on a perch, the lonely post

Raging Dove

There's a way to walk this line
It's not pleasant or very sweet
Picking yourself off the floor
Get movement to your feet
Don't look both ways to cross
Ignore the warning alarms
Set a pace to get back home
Include the flailing arms
The path will narrow some
Stepping up to the race
It's all downhill at the end
Forgive the frantic pace
You've been here before
It's what you know and love
Home is where the heart is
Courage of the raging dove
In the mind you will anguish
Yet peace reigns over pain
Vengeance is best served
As you show great restrain
It's a life not fit for most
As they can't handle it
They lend a goodly ear

Then continue on their sit
Get movement to the heart
Fight through as if it's fine
You'll thank me someday
There's a way to walk this line

(12-23-2012)

Raging
Dove

There's a way to walk this line
It's not pleasant or very sweet
Picking yourself off the floor
Get movement to your feet
Don't look both ways to cross
Ignore the warning alarms
Set a pace to get back home
Include the flailing arms
The path will narrow some
Stepping up to the race
It's all downhill at the end
Forgive the frantic pace
You've been here before
It's what you know and love
Home is where the heart is
Courage of the raging dove
In the mind you will anguish
Yet peace reigns over pain
Vengeance is best served
As you show great restrain
It's a life not fit for most
As they can't handle it
They lend a goodly ear
Then continue on their sit
Get movement to the heart
Fight through as if it's fine
You'll thank me someday
There's a way to walk this line

Wm Koch Jr.   12-23-2012

Homage

HOMAGE

hom·age noun \ˈä-mij, ˈhä-\

: Respect or honor

: Something that is done to honor someone or something

Full Definition of Homage

1. a: a feudal ceremony by which a man acknowledges
    himself the vassal of a lord
    b: the relationship between a feudal lord and his vassal
    c: an act done or payment made in meeting the
    obligations of vassalage

2. a: expression of high regard: Respect—often used
    with pay
    b: something that shows respect or attests to the worth
    or influence of another : Tribute <his long life filled
    with international homage's to his unique musical
    talent

Examples of Homage

*   Her book is a *homage* to her favorite city.

*   <the poem is a moving *homage* to all who have
    served in our nation's armed services>

Origin of Homage

Middle English, from Anglo-French homage, omage, from home man, vassal, from Latin homin-, homo human being; akin to Old English guma human being, Latin humus earth —more at humble

First Known Use: 14th century

Related to Homage

Synonyms

accolade, citation, commendation, dithyramb, eulogium, eulogy, encomium, hymn, paean, panegyric, salutation, tribute

> America the Beautiful
> America! America!
> God shed his grace on thee
> And crown thy good with brotherhood
> From sea to shining sea!

Words by Katharine Lee Bates

Bleeding Red

Waters smooth then rocky rough
People worn till they had enough
Shed of tears, misplacing grace
Losing focus on the Lord's place
Good and bad, spirit stays true
Bleeding red with white and blue
America, a nation's harkened call
All gave some while some gave all
Rich of resource and soul of man
Amen, so part of each American
Dedication duty and guiding light
Freedom fought with every fight
Warriors mission, clear the path
Good works flow, without the wrath
Loyal to oath, salute to "Old Glory"
Founder's ideals, tell the real story
Brotherhood of man, noble in deed
Direction from the Father, still a need
Blessing a people with helping hand
Battle for souls across a great land
Conscience effort to live and love
Under protection from high above
Reach to open minds and each heart
United States began with this start
Humble children to listen and learn

Wandered off, now due to return
Claim his grace he shed on thee
America lives sea to shining sea
Sacred heart that's given to you
Bleeding red with white and blue

(3-24-2012)

A Beautiful Face

Behold the beauty and the kind
Characters and traits desired to find
Often the pretty shall be vain at hand
As compassion is rarer across the land

Combine those into a mix of appeal
An innocent angel with a caring zeal
Passion and soul of an eternal heart
Lost to the ages, now a sorrow depart

Concern for the animals in man's trust
Mother the abandoned left in the dust
Putting others ahead of the price to pay
Forging sympathy each and every day

Qualities of a saint dispersed to heaven
Watch all from above twenty four seven
To find the desired character and traits
Look no further then the golden gates

Behold the beauty and the kind
Characters and traits desired to find
Rare the pretty shall carry with grace
Compassion complete, a beautiful face

(5-12-2013)

A Beautiful Face

Behold the beauty and the kind
Characters and traits desired to find
Often the pretty shall be vain at hand
As compassion is rarer across the land

Combine those into a mix of appeal
An innocent angel with a caring zeal
Passion and soul of an eternal heart
Lost to the ages, now a sorrow depart

Concern for the animals in man's trust
Mother the abandoned left in the dust
Putting others ahead of the price to pay
Forging sympathy each and every day

Qualities of a saint dispersed to heaven
Watch all from above twenty four seven
To find the desired character and traits
Look no further then the golden gates

Behold the beauty and the kind
Characters and traits desired to find
Rare the pretty shall carry with grace
Compassion complete, a beautiful face

Wm Koch Jr.
5-12-2013©

Without a Sound

Alone I write
Recluse and blue
Quiet of heart
Awake on cue
Dark, no light
Without a sound
Eternal flight
Rumble ground
Howl of wind
Beckons dreams
Moonlight shine
Neighing screams
Escape the woods
Break free at last
Run wild away
Forget the past
Spirit of love
Gallops away
Pursuit behind
Yesterday
Light of dark
Speed tonight

Breaking reins
Stampeding plight
Roaming free
Fields abound
Expressing hope
Without a sound

(4-27-2012)

Without a Sound

Alone I write
Recluse and blue
Quiet of heart
Awake on cue
Dark, no light
Without a sound
Eternal flight
Rumble ground
Howl of wind
Beckons dreams
Moonlight shine
Neighing screams
Escape the woods
Break free at last
Run wild away
Forget the past
Spirit of love
Gallops away
Pursuit behind
Yesterday
Light of dark
Speed tonight
Breaking reins
Stampeding plight
Roaming free
Fields abound
Expressing hope
Without a sound

© Wm Koch Jr.
4-27-2012

William Koch Jr.

Last Call

Standing firm for the last call
All gave some, some gave all
Tribute to the defending guard
Nothing's easy when it is so hard
Protect freedom for many to share
Sentinels of justice, none to spare
Tribute to them in pomp and post
Flowing honor in form of the toast

Standing firm for the last call
Recognize their medals on the wall
Citations are not why they go to war
Only reward is to come home from tour
Battered and bruised can heal itself
Coins and awards still sit the shelf
Wounds of severe nature take a toll
Service of duty was the only goal

Standing firm for the last call
Wounds of life but not the fall
Silver Star families become a count
Anger and frustration surely mount
Living remembrance of a tragic pain
One that also never loses its strain
Courage and hope forever appealed
Captured only by emotions revealed

Standing firm for the last call
Attention to the shadow so tall
Support the troops at every cost
Fallen Heroes and families of the lost
Wounded Warriors that need a hand
Protecting freedom and America's land
Saying they did their job, that is all
Standing firm for the last call

(11-6-2011)

My Walk

My walk is slow
It begs to end
Sore of feet
Life to spend
Little to feel
Or touch bestow
Wind shutters cold
Losing its flow
Sight is weak
As vision fades
Colors blurred
Spectacle aids
A scent of loss
Aroma of love
Aloft to heaven
So high above
Ache from sleep
Restless time
Words erupt
Tribute rhyme
Whispered dreams
Hear the call
Accolade brave
Honor the Fall
Sorrowful days

Broken of heart
Travel a path
Serving a part
Spending life
As soul, so sore
Endless begging
My walk, some more

(6-2-2012)

A Soul of Worth

Each life is priceless
Money beyond the earth
Treasure each journey
Searching, a soul of worth

Give no quarter
Fear not a dime
Cast every nickel
A "cent" of rhyme

Notes of the buck
Five to every ten
Twenty is a score
A fifty, yet when

Hundred reasons why
By paper and iron ore
Slips between fingers
Having less is more

Cash may be king
With it or without
Earning or learning
Mass market about

Work is a pathway
You spend or save
Never get to keep
What anyone gave

Now, a scent of rhyme
Just one of the five
Count every blessing
While you are alive

Each life is priceless
Money beyond the earth
Treasure each journey
Found, a soul of worth

(7-3-2014)

A Soul of Worth

Wm Koch Jr. 7-3-2014©

Each life is priceless
Money beyond the earth
Treasure each journey
Searching, a soul of worth

Give no quarter
Fear not a dime
Cast every nickel
A "cent" of rhyme

Notes of the buck
Five to every ten
Twenty is a score
A fifty, yet when

Hundred reasons why
By paper and iron ore
Slips between fingers
Having less is more

Cash may be king
With it or without
Earning or learning
Mass market about

Work is a pathway
You spend or save
Never get to keep
What anyone gave

Now, a scent of rhyme
Just one of the five
Count every blessing
While you are alive

Each life is priceless
Money beyond the earth
Treasure each journey
Found, a soul of worth

Loyal to the Past

In reflection of a lonely goal
Search blindly the broken soul
As the slow of a starving fast
Stands ever loyal to the past

Brought to knees in agony pain
Refuse healing with image vain
No amends to a desperate plea
Nothing comforts a lonely thee

Resist and defy the giving love
Hurled down from an angel dove
Any hope for relief tomorrow
Forever lost in present sorrow

A fight is on as the light goes out
Keep silent still through the shout
Talk is cheap and does little good
Expecting more then what it could

Present leads back to the past
First in line is always the last
Honored true and honored blue
Medals and portraits are the clue

The march that leads to the gold
Of warrior battles lonesome cold

Scars that will never see the light
Remembrance of the glory fight

Search blindly the broken soul
In reflection of a lonely goal
Of heroic name in the stone cast
Stands ever loyal to the past

(5-12-2014)

Loyal to
the Past

Wm Koch Jr.   5-12-2014©

In reflection of a lonely goal
Search blindly the broken soul
As the slow of a starving fast
Stands ever loyal to the past
Brought to knees in agony pain
Refuse healing with image vain
No amends to a desperate plea
Nothing comforts a lonely thee
Resist and defy the giving love
Hurled down from an angel dove
Any hope for relief tomorrow
Forever lost in present sorrow
A fight is on as the light goes out
Keep silent still through the shout
Talk is cheap and does little good
Expecting more then what it could
Present leads back to the past
First in line is always the last
Honored true and honored blue
Medals and portraits are the clue
The march that leads to the gold
Of warrior battles lonesome cold
Scars that will never see the light
Remembrance of the glory fight
Search blindly the broken soul
In reflection of a lonely goal
Of heroic name in the stone cast
Stands ever loyal to the past

Standing Yet

Structure of hope, corner of life
Weakened strength of painful strife
Base succumbs to a tragic forecast
Fallen all around, I guess I'm the last

Hollow walls of foundation remain
Strong once, shall never be the same
Silent in strength, unpainted face
Standing yet, abandoned in place

Old and worn thin to the very cores
Cold wind blows thru forgotten doors
Not able to stay warm or market dreams
Shutter up the sound of agony screams

Hard wood floors that are left for dust
Memories run, but remember I must
Struggle to rebuild what's left behind
Show I am still one of a certain kind

Protecting others, the structure of hope
Forge new strength, gather aid to cope
Fight the decay that comes with time
Façade of each day hides in the rhyme

Old and worn, looks beyond my years
Aging lines brought on with the tears
Silent in strength, unpainted face
Standing yet, abandoned in place

(4-21-2012)

A Book

A book discarded for years
Sullen and quiet; it appears
Knowledge able ready to find
Turning loose a hungry mind

Words together in an order
Knows no mindful border
Imagination open to skies
Sorrow tales of many cries

Fables that whisk you away
Troubles of a painful day
Love stories told to adore
Lusting for so much more

Information made to expand
Revelations to an open hand
Volumes dusted off to expose
Feelings never able to close

Verses that make you reflect
Of honor and patriotic respect
Written to create good feelings
Composed to seek real healings

Cover closed to those that stare
Springs open for many that care

Stand alone but together in stacks
Words of writers, poets and hacks

Ideas, images and of lost love
Guidance from a light above
Sullen and quiet, in tears
A book discarded for years

(2-25-2012)

Be Enough

Will it ever be enough
Holding love so tough
In hope and some dreams
Muffled cries or screams

Will it ever be enough
Kiss a knee seeing scuff
With toys in the yard
Through schools so hard

Will it ever be enough
Growing up seems rough
Games to past the time
Write or reading rhyme

Will it ever be enough
Childhood to teenage stuff
Boys and jobs to impress
Beaches and a party dress

Will it ever be enough
Work blouse with a cuff
Bright as a summer day
Longing for a way to stay

Will it ever be enough
Smoke in a magic puff
Disappear in the free air
Calming the common fear

Will it ever be enough
Past the stage of the gruff
Of boys of each brother
A sister like a mother

Will it ever be enough
Holding love so tough
In hope and some dreams
Muffled cries or screams

(4-29-2013)

Be Enough

Will it ever be enough
Holding love so tough
In hope and some dreams
Muffled cries or screams

Will it ever be enough
Kiss a knee seeing scuff
With toys in the yard
Through schools so hard

Will it ever be enough
Growing up seems rough
Games to past the time
Write or reading rhyme

Will it ever be enough
Childhood to teenage stuff
Boys and jobs to impress
Beaches and a party dress

Will it ever be enough
Work blouse with a cuff
Bright as a summer day
Longing for a way to stay

Will it ever be enough
Smoke in a magic puff
Disappear in the free air
Calming the common fear

Will it ever be enough
Past the stage of the gruff
Of boys of each brother
A sister like a mother

Will it ever be enough
Holding love so tough
In hope and some dreams
Muffled cries or screams

Wm. Koch Jr.
4-29-2013

Heroes We Make

Toys and boys
Socks with rocks
Girls in curls
Hair with flair
Children you raise
In starry eye gaze
Hopes and a dream
A family, a team
Balls and falls
Cuts from ruts
Names of games
Hikes with bikes
Each life, each child
Tame or some wild
Prepare for the world
A story unfurled
Teens on scenes
Flirts in skirts
Sports with shorts
Pals with gals
The worry, the wait
A door or a gate
Late night arrives
Free wheel drives
Schools or tools

Trades with grades
College for knowledge
Shirk or work
Release and the pride
Parents fear can't hide
Passed what you knew
Doing all you can do
Sons toting guns
Camo with ammo
Share and care
Fears to tears
Children are lost
Freedom's cost
Path they take
Heroes we make

(8-1-2012)

Heroes We Make

Wm Koch Jr.
5-1-2019

Toys and boys
Socks with rocks
Girls in curls
Hair with flair
Children you raise
In starry eye gaze
Hopes and a dream
A family, a team

Balls and falls
Cuts from ruts
Names of games
Hikes with bikes
Each life, each child
Tame or some wild
Prepare for the world
A story unfurled

Teens on scenes
Flirts in skirts
Sports with shorts
Pals with gals
The worry, the wait
A door or a gate
Late night arrives
Free wheel drives

Schools or tools
Trades with grades
College for knowledge
Shirk or work
Release and the pride
Parents fear can't hide
Passed what you knew
Doing all you can do

Sons toting guns
Camo with ammo
Share and care
Fears to tears
Children are lost
Freedoms' cost
Path they take
Heroes we make

Loyal

LOYAL

loy·aladjective \'loï(-ə)l\
: having or showing complete and constant support for someone or something

Full Definition of Loyal

1. unswerving in allegiance: as
    a: faithful in allegiance to one's lawful sovereign or government
    b: faithful to a private person to whom fidelity is due
    c: faithful to a cause, ideal, custom, institution, or product

2. showing loyalty

3. obsolete: lawful, legitimate

loy·al·ly \'loï-ə-lē\adverb

Examples of Loyal

- The team has many *loyal* fans.

- She has provided the company with many years of *loyal* service.

Origin of Loyal

Middle French, from Old French leial, leel, from Latin legalis legal

First Known Use: 1531

Related to Loyal

Synonyms

constant, dedicated, devoted, devout, down-the-line, fast, good, faithful, pious, staunch (also stanch), steadfast, steady, true, true-blue

Quiet

Quiet now
Say not a word
I've come for the past
Is it all I have heard
No tears as I walk away
Calm, you'll get your day
I won't be there to see
But you'll remember me

Quiet be still
You'll see I was right
Dreams are broken
Dark is the night
A path to follow behind
Led by the noble kind
I won't be there to see
But you'll remember me

Quiet evermore
In honor to the end
Ashes spread about
Nothing left to defend
Spirit rules the day
With plenty left to say
I won't be there to see
But you'll remember me

Quiet
Not a sound
Peace is restful silence
Above and below ground
Memories have their pain
History is the strain
I won't be there to see
Will you remember me

(1-25-2012)

Quiet

Quiet now
Say not a word
I've come for the past
Is it all I have heard
No tears as I walk away
Calm, you'll get your day
I won't be there to see
But you'll remember me

Quiet be still
You'll see I was right
Dreams are broken
Dark is the night
A path to follow behind
Led by the noble kind
I won't be there to see
But you'll remember me

Quiet evermore
In honor to the end
Ashes spread about
Nothing left to defend
Spirit rules the day
With plenty left to say
I won't be there to see
But you'll remember me

Quiet
Not a sound
Peace is restful silence
Above and below ground
Memories have their pain
History is the strain
I won't be there to see
Will you remember me

Wm Kosh Jr.   1-25-2012

Never a Day

Boots worn of sacrifice
Black of troops aground
Muddy, bloody and ice
Round by brutal round

Laced with courage tight
Eyelets of vision pure
March forward to fight
Searching for the cure

Dedication of the heart
A sight of an eagle eye
Deployment far apart
Families left to cry

Soldiers of silent sorrow
Filled their plotted lot
Look back at tomorrow
Restless of a hallow cot

Sister, mother or brothers
Father, daughter, a child
Family, friends or others
Emotions that are wild

Forgotten, never a day
Spirits in many a word
Freedom of the fire fray
Justice that they heard

Boots worn of sacrifice
Bronzed of troops brave
Medals, ribbons of a price
Ultimate cost they gave

(3-10-2013)

Never a Day

Boots worn of sacrifice
Black of troops aground
Muddy, bloody and ice
Round by brutal round

Laced with courage tight
Eyelets of vision pure
March forward to fight
Searching for the cure

Dedication of the heart
A sight of an eagle eye
Deployment far apart
Families left to cry

Soldiers of silent sorrow
Filled their plotted lot
Look back at tomorrow
Restless of a hallow cot

Sister, mother or brothers
Father, daughter, a child
Family, friends or others
Emotions that are wild

Forgotten, never a day
Spirits in many a word
Freedom of the fire fray
Justice that they heard

Boots worn of sacrifice
Bronzed of troops brave
Medals, ribbons of a price
Ultimate cost they gave

Wm Koch Jr.
3-10-2013©

Retired Number

Just one of many that took the oath to liberty serve
Of diverse backgrounds that show the humble nerve
Sovereign sons of American pride that's number one
Dearest daughters with camo that trains with a gun
Brave mothers protecting a nation beyond family ties
Gallant fathers making sure safe, are children's eyes
Brothers that take the lead to the dangerous point
Sisters are defenders along with a heavenly anoint

Fighting as one for liberty and a great common cause
Show courage with compassion and tribute the pause
There are no parades or accolades for them my friend
Besides their family and a few that's where it will end
No paper or news carries the story of valor under fire
Few write or will produce a show that honors a retire
There's very little remembrance of the guts or the glory
Followed closely behind by no fanfare to a heroic story

They volunteered to uphold a virtue of freedom and rights
Patrol and converge come daylight or the darken nights
Branch colors are of the bold and never a day will run
In the knowledge they wave continually, under the sun
Stadiums will fill for a sport or a team that lacks success
Fans pile in to applaud or tailgate in an extreme excess

Music will drift from concerts till the
hours of a gentle slumber
Yet there be no following for an old soldier's retired number

(7-31-2013)

Retired Number

Just one of many that took the oath to liberty serve
Of diverse backgrounds that show the humble nerve
Sovereign sons of American pride that's number one
Dearest daughters with camo that trains with a gun
Brave mothers protecting a nation beyond family ties
Gallant fathers making sure safe, are children's eyes
Brothers that take the lead to the dangerous point
Sisters are defenders along with a heavenly anoint

Fighting as one for liberty and a great common cause
Show courage with compassion and tribute the pause
There are no parades or accolades for them my friend
Besides their family and a few that's where it will end
No paper or news carries the story of valor under fire
Few write or will produce a show that honors a retire
There's very little remembrance of the guts or the glory
Followed closely behind by no fanfare to a heroic story

They volunteered to uphold a virtue of freedom and rights
Patrol and converge come daylight or the darken nights
Branch colors are of the bold and never a day will run
In the knowledge they wave continually, under the sun
Stadiums will fill for a sport or a team that lacks success
Fans pile in to applaud or tailgate in an extreme excess
Music will drift from concerts till the hours of a gentle slumber
Yet there be no following for an old soldiers' retired number

Wm Koch Jr.   7-31-2013

Courage of the Heart

Courage of the heart
Not always plain to see
Blends character and care
Many ways it can be

Brave to give of yourself
Another trait of nerve
Life for many others
Heroes of golden serve

Attribute of compassion
Another way to guide
Sacrifice self interest
Never leaves to hide

Courage in the blood
Ready at all stands
Overflowing trust
Of faithful duty hands

A bond of brilliance
Shining in the dark
Power of the persona
Imagery is so stark

To walk the walk
Without much ado
Sense of lasting days
Knowing, I love you

Many ways of care
Each a valuable part
Not always plain to see
Courage of the heart

(7-24-2012)

Newsprint Cries

Newsprint cries out in black and white
With joyous occasions by day or night
Of events that can spread much ado
Or small spaces of those feeling blue

It's here that some will miss their chance
To announce a wedding or magic romance
For their love one has now been lost
There is so much more to a fatal cost

As families share their hopes and dreams
It's the lost ones, which dread the screams
Of silent nature, yet pain for all of their time
Retold in the colors of the sorrowful rhyme

There is no happy event for them to thus tell
Your heroes gone off to war and bravely fell
Or came home with wounds aplenty but unseen
Pleasure thoughts of words are now on the lean

Restless families feel the constant stress
No celebrations in a tuxedo or party dress
It's not even easy to read of all the others
Losing daughters along with their brothers

Fathers have also fallen, more than just one
Mom's of love ones, nowhere to now run
Yet, no words can write a good truthful try
For any type setter will be reduced to a cry

It's the knowledge of no future good times
No toast of soco shots with slices of limes
Planning and details lay cold on the floor
There's no festival to travel for, anymore

Now notices placed as memorial tributes
Are the only kinds of the printed salutes
With joyous occasions now far out of sight
Newsprint cries out in black and white

(10-15-2012)

I Stand

I stand, there for I am alive
The route of the present drive
Where turns left or to the right
Leave me alone against the fight

I stood, that's where it will end
Of honor, tribute and to defend
Whatever happens to me now
Questions persist of where and how

Understand, I have the will to go
Moving through what I now know
Falling into the façade of a dream
All for one and one for the team

Understood, there's no there, there
Mattering less is no one will care
A path shall be neither left nor right
Leave me alone, against the fight

Misunderstand, I've said too much
Remaining yet, the poets touch
Where word order is the only feel
Awareness out, yet little heal

Misunderstood, please have no doubt
My dedication to tribute will be out
Taking me against the left and right
Leaves me alone against the fight

(10-16-2013)

A Guiding Way

Open your eyes to life
Close your mind to strife
A child is born this day
For a later price to pay
Coming to play and learn
For a sacrifice at his turn
To know him, is to love him
Living a life full to the brim
Caring for others so much
Plain to see, his reaching touch
Goes forth to protect from harm
A smirk of a smile as his charm
Leading by action and noble deeds
With a platoon that follow his leads
He now shows a soul to behold
A Fallen Hero that is truly gold
Not perfect, but no one can be
One of many heroes, not just to me
I honor and tribute him this day
To my youngest son's 27th birthday
Your presence in my mind reveals
My heart break of sorrow appeals
That you fought for others at war
Your loss results, our family of tore

So many calls for us to move onward
Sorry, they miss the call that we heard
Many more ask how we get through
In truth the answer "I wish I knew"
When a child leaves to take control
Parents and siblings know their roll
To support them to the end of days
That sacrifice that a few only pays
A child is born this day
My son of a guiding way

(10-25-2011)

A Patriotic Sleep

Waking from a quiet sleep
A sleep of dedicated eyes
Searching for the blue
Blue stars of open skies
Where white clouds mix
Mix with the sun set red
Clear in the far off horizon
Soul and liberty just ahead

A soul of values and trust
Trust of founders laws
Justice binds us together
Under eagle peaceful claws
A republic in freedom's name
United the States to the end
Rights of her men and women
With principles left to defend

Of liberty that we shall live
Live through night and day
Protect those less fortunate
Provide a patriot's final pay

White stars of spacious skies
Red sun sets in blue sky deep
Opening from my closed eyes
Waking from a patriotic sleep

(2-26-2013)

Majestic in Beauty

Flag of my father
Carried by a son
Pride of America
Colors never run

Scarlet of sacrifice
Fight of the brave
Heroes to humble
Lives that they gave

Banner of justice
Power of restraint
Clothe of kinship
Savior to the faint

White of passion
Liberty's heartbeat
Republic of the people
Constitutional seat

Flag of my country
Majestic in beauty
Hope for the world
Waves for all to see

Blue in loyalty
A solemn decree
Fight injustice
Sea to shining sea

Standard bearing
Freedom of choice
Land opportunities
People's open voice

Red white and blue
Stars of each state
The eternal America
Trust in its fate

Majestic in Beauty

Flag of my father
Carried by a son
Pride of America
Colors never run

Scarlet of sacrifice
Fight of the brave
Heroes to humble
Lives that they gave

Banner of justice
Power of restraint
Clothe of kinship
Savior to the faint

White of passion
Liberty's heartbeat
Republic of the people
Constitutional seat

Flag of my country
Majestic in beauty
Hope for the world
Waves for all to see

Blue in loyalty
A solemn decree
Fight injustice
Sea to shining sea

Standard bearing
Freedom of choice
Land opportunities
People's open voice

Red white and blue
Stars of each state
The eternal America
Trust in its' fate

Compassion Colors

If you could see compassion, what colors would they be
In apple red with navy blue, white does it just for me
Is it majestic purple of royal, to comfort all the ills
A gallant green of infantry, to lead up story hills
Precious gold of heart, the hero and waving hair
Silver of the elders, which brings the gentle tear
Bronze is always the bold, yet cold to the touch
Black or gray tones lonely, caring loses so very much
Orange and yellow bright, upbeat yet not a care
Brown to the Auburn, presents the sullen stare
Compassion colors exist; I've seen them all before
Multitude of the bands, as much as you can store
Far in the distance, though better as they near
Seeing is believing, the picture is crystal clear
Compassion weathered old, more a feeling then a hue
Through thin and the thick, emotions of righteous true
Caring starts with learning, the importance of one life
Comfort those needing aid, relieve their battle strife
In apple red with navy blue, white does it just for me
If you could see compassion, what colors would they be

(3-28-2014)

Compassion Colors

If you could see compassion, what colors would they be
In apple red with navy blue, white does it just for me
Is it majestic purple of royal, to comfort all the ills
A gallant green of infantry, to lead up story hills
Precious gold of heart, the hero and waving hair
Silver of the elders, which brings the gentle tear
Bronze is always the bold, yet cold to the touch
Black or gray tones lonely, caring loses so very much
Orange and yellow bright, upbeat yet not a care
Brown to the Auburn, presents the sullen stare

Compassion colors exist; I've seen them all before
Multitude of the bands, as much as you can store
Far in the distance, though better as they near
Seeing is believing, the picture is crystal clear
Compassion weathered old, more a feeling then a hue
Through thin and the thick, emotions of righteous true
Caring starts with learning, the importance of one life
Comfort those needing aid, relieve their battle strife
In apple red with navy blue, white does it just for me
If you could see compassion, what colors would they be

Wm Koch Jr.   3-28-2014

Battle of Yesterday

As smoke has cleared, the musket seems old
Embers of the fire, with ashes running cold
Battle of yesterday, of the spirit of yore
Turned to a debate, who's keeping score

Brother against brother, the blood of each field
Freedom or slavery, each side seeking yield
A battle of yesterday, for liberty at her best
Rights of self rule, captivity for the rest

War on each horizon, a world at the brink
Bombs from the air, ships afloat shall sink
Battle of yesterday, oppression defeated
Flags of victory, have now all retreated

South of each line, divides each country
Americans serve brave, with lives the fee
Battle of yesterday, turning to the red
Not just the fields, conscience of the head

Winds turn cold, with arms at each side
Eyes in the sky, nowhere to now hide
Battle of yesterday, tyranny is broke
Back with vengeance, rights now a joke

History will record, how America unites
To save liberty, embers of the fights

Battle of yesterday, now your front yard
Voting to restore, reverence of the guard

Sacrifice by the ages, a spirit of the free
Concord to Gettysburg, landing at Normandy
Battle of yesterday, Vietnam, Iraq, and Kabul
Will the Spirit of 1776, be wasted on us all

(10-13-2012)

As smoke has cleared, the musket seems old
Embers' of the fire, with ashes running cold
Battle of yesterday, of the spirit of yore
Turned to a debate, who's keeping score

Brother against brother, the blood of each field
Freedom or slavery, each side seeking yield
A battle of yesterday, for liberty at her best
Rights of self rule, captivity for the rest

War on each horizon, a world at the brink
Bombs from the air, ships afloat shall sink
Battle of yesterday, oppression defeated
Flags of victory, have now all retreated

South of each line, divides each country
Americans serve brave, with lives the fee
Battle of yesterday, turning to the red
Not just the fields, conscience of the head

Winds turn cold, with arms at each side
Eyes in the sky, nowhere to now hide
Battle of yesterday, tyranny is broke
Back with vengeance, rights now a joke

History will record, how America unites
To save liberty, embers of the fights
Battle of yesterday, now your front yard
Voting to restore, reverence of the gnard

Sacrifice by the ages, a spirit of the free
Concord to Gettysburg, landing at Normandy
Battle of yesterday, Vietnam, Iraq and Kabul
Will the Spirit of 1776, be wasted on us all

Wm Koch Jr.
10-13-2012ª

Battle of Yesterday

Sullen

SULLEN

sul·len adjective \'sə-lən\

: Used to describe an angry or unhappy person who does not want to talk, smile, etc.

: Gray and dark

Full Definition of Sullen

1. a: gloomily or resentfully silent or repressed <a sullen crowd>

   b: suggesting a sullen state : lowering <a sullen countenance>

2. dull or somber in sound or color

3. dismal, gloomy <a sullen morning>

4. moving sluggishly <a sullen river>
   sul·len·ly adverb
   sul·len·ness \'sə-lə(n)-nəs\noun

Examples of Sullen

- <*sullen* skies that matched our mood on the day of the funeral>

- <*sullen* and bored at his in-laws' house, he couldn't wait for the holidays to end>

Origin of Sullen

Middle English solein solitary, from Anglo-French sulein, solain, perhaps from sol, soul single, sole + -ain after Old French soltain solitary, private, from Late Latin solitaneus, ultimately from Latin solus alone

First Known Use: 14th century

Related to Sullen

Synonyms

black, bleak, cheerless, chill, cloudy, cold, comfortless, dark, darkening, depressing, depressive, desolate, dire, disconsolate, dismal, drear, dreary, glum, godforsaken, gray, lonely, lonesome,miserable, morbid, morose, solemn, somber, gloomy, wretched

My Front Door

Turning to a knock at my front door
Knowing there's no way to take anymore
No dust has settled on my broken heart
To be shaken off for sorrows restart
The pain that carry's through each day
Leaves very little room for a life today
Hours peak each day's night of the dark
Begin again with each morning dogs' bark
Sleep would be a welcome friend in deed
Nightmares of past thoughts forever bleed
Remaining a feeling that there is more
Turning to a knock at my front door
No rest for the weary is a known fact
But agony of lost love leaves you to act
A façade that is worn to cover the soul
May fool some, even when most is the goal
Cold settles in to take a spot at your side
Memories of your life, that are hard to hide
I repeat the silence of screams that roar
Turning to a knock at my front door

(10-21-2011)

Loving Died

My mind drifts away
To a tragic kind of day
Where loving left to die
Leaving me to forever cry
A lady of caring respect
Of now my gentle reflect
The day my loving died
Oh how, the people cried

Family and friends are lost
Brother rock, knows the cost
She left for a warriors love
Now united as soldiers above
A woman of true compassion
From a heart's forever bastion
The day my loving died
Of course, the angels cried

Fragile are thoughts across
Overcome by a tragic loss
Her touch of loving soul
Continues her eternal goal
A lady of caring respect
Of now my gentle reflect
The day my loving died
Oh how, the people cried

I beg for relief of sorrow
Pray to end my tomorrow
From the ache of my heart
Pleading for my depart
A child in honor of loyal
Daughter of tribute royal
The day my loving died
Forever, this father cried

(7-4-2012)

Loving Died

My mind drifts away
To a tragic kind of day
Where loving left to die
Leaving me to forever cry
A lady of caring respect
Of now my gentle reflect
The day my loving died
Oh how, the people cried

Family and friends are lost
Brother rock, knows the cost
She left for a warriors love
Now united as soldiers above
A woman of true compassion
From a hearts' forever bastion
The day my loving died
Of course, the angels cried

Fragile are thoughts across
Overcome by a tragic loss
Her touch of loving soul
Continues her eternal goal
A lady of caring respect
Of now my gentle reflect
The day my loving died
Oh how, the people cried

I beg for relief of sorrow
Pray to end my tomorrow
From the ache of my heart
Pleading for my depart
A child in honor of loyal
Daughter of tribute royal
The day my loving died
Forever, this father cried

Wm Koch Jr.
7-4-2012©

Cupboard of Ware

A house quiet, barren of any sound
Missing are sights, none to be found
Of children laughing and busy with sport
No grandparents holding thanksgiving court

Aroma of a feast, in memories of old
Vanished into thin air, of autumn cold
Table set with plates in holiday fun
Empty chairs count as a daughter and son

Cupboard of ware, standing at the guard
Place sets now amiss, remembering is hard
As food and faith as dinner forever served
Golden are the moments in time preserved

Spirits of both, the lonely and of the wine
A family tradition, engrained as now mine
With giving as emotions of many a thanks
Sacrifice or compassion has lessened our ranks

Each day is a blessing, to those so alive
Getting through a holiday, is just to survive
Of children present and busy with beautiful life
Thanksgiving memories without the strife

Cupboard of ware, behind clear glass panes
Place sets now amiss, stacked in memory lanes
As food and faith nourish the heart and soul
Golden are the moments, a Thanksgiving's goal

(Thanksgiving, 11-28-2013)

Cupboard of Ware

Wm Koch Jr.
Thanksgiving 11-28-2013©

A house quiet, barren of any sound
Missing are sights, none to be found
Of children laughing and busy with sport
No grandparents holding thanksgiving court

Aroma of a feast, in memories of old
Vanished into thin air, of autumn cold
Table set with plates in holiday fun
Empty chairs count as a daughter and son

Cupboard of ware, standing at the guard
Place sets now amiss, remembering is hard
As food and faith as dinner forever served
Golden are the moments in time preserved

Spirits of both, the lonely and of the wine
A family tradition, engrained as now mine
With giving as emotions of many a thanks
Sacrifice or compassion has lessened our ranks

Each day is a blessing, to those so alive
Getting through a holiday, is just to survive
Of children present and busy with beautiful life
Thanksgiving memories without the strife

Cupboard of ware, behind clear glass panes
Place sets now amiss, stacked in memory lanes
As food and faith nourish the heart and soul
Golden are the moments, a Thanksgivings goal

Weakened Knee

Each knee is weakened
I can't go very far
A path of cold and hard
Concrete or blackened tar

Filled with thorn of brush
Rocky hill into decline
Past the pillars of fire
Cross the judgment line

There still is some hope
With angels due to call
Lift me fast over head
Past every tearful fall

As age catches up to me
I've slowed down some
Look ever forward fresh
Wait thy kingdom come

Each day brings anew
Obstacles in my path
Memories go the distance
Wash away the wrath

The sun shines down bright
As clouds part gently away
Breaking of the dark night
Enlightens past yesterday

A day in the far horizon
Which I can't really see
Of a agony journey ahead
One with a weakened knee

(5-6-2013)

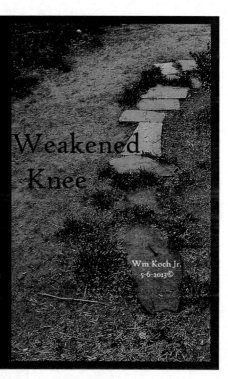

Each knee is weakened
I can't go very far
A path of cold and hard
Concrete or blackened tar

Filled with thorn of brush
Rocky hill into decline
Past the pillars of fire
Cross the judgment line

There still is some hope
With angels due to call
Lift me fast over head
Past every tearful fall

As age catches up to me
I've slowed down some
Look ever forward fresh
Wait thy kingdom come

Each day brings anew
Obstacles in my path
Memories go the distance
Wash away the wrath

The sun shines down bright
As clouds part gently away
Breaking of the dark night
Enlightens past yesterday

A day in the far horizon
Which I can't really see
Of a agony journey ahead
One with a weakened knee

Weakened Knee

Wm Koch Jr.
5-6-2013©

Compartments of the Heart

Placing a hand over my heart
Can't help think of every part
Different levels with doors each
Loves compartments, out of reach
For family of those younger years
Others flow with some tender tears
Love to children that doesn't close
A unique one for your special rose
Doors of keyed numbered locks
Often broken down or up on blocks
Some are empty or abandoned too
Misplaced keys, what's a heart to do
Starting over in love can cause strain
Losing those loved, providing the pain
Places of dark issues along with the light
Sections of peace or the internal fight
It makes no difference where you are
Absent of love, is a love much too far
Precious are the parts that live a life
Harden like coal, the ones of strife
Placing my hand, over this heartache
Can't help think of my livable sake
Different levels of sorrow to store
Loves compartments, wanting more

(5-26-2012)

Spiral Staircase

The spiral staircase
Steps in the round
Slowly you shall pace
Feel no solid ground
Circle of malcontent
Unleveled and steep
It's where I reside
With very little sleep
Rising to new heights
Of iron metal and cold
Dropping to low depths
Broken hearted and old
Railings of sharp razors
Cutting hands to a shred
Letting go blindly in pain
Visions of my agony head
Descending farther down
Trampled onto the floor
Hitting the rock bottom
Searching for a door
Arising to then stand
Left over the right
Starting right back up
Every single night
Ascend from the ground

A walk much too fast
Round on top of round
Spiral staircase to ever last

(8-19-2012)

River of Remorse

The river of remorse
Flow gentle as a stream
Calm and slow trickle
Forming like a dream

Emotion lightly afloat
Carries hope eternally
Past rapids of hardship
Over hazards not to see

Wade to the deep end
As waters rise from haste
Troubles gather rhythm
Vantage goes to waste

Regrets and revelations
The river of remorse
Bending from the vision
Unsteady in its course

Rushing cascades racing
Tides flood the mind caves
Fighting back the current
Battling against the waves

Overcome by the swiftness
Waters of constant strain
Forever weary to a rest
Eroding none of the pain

Guided by the notion
Survival is the source
Gasping for the saving
The river of remorse

(8-2-2014)

The river of remorse
Flow gentle as a stream
Calm and slow trickle
Forming like a dream

Rushing cascades racing
Tides flood the mind caves
Fighting back the current
Battling against the waves

Emotion lightly afloat
Carries hope eternally
Past rapids of hardship
Over hazards not to see

Overcome by the swiftness
Waters of constant strain
Forever weary to a rest
Eroding none of the pain

Wade to the deep end
As waters rise from haste
Troubles gather rhythm
Vantage goes to waste

Guided by the notion
Survival is the source
Gasping for the saving
The river of remorse

Regrets and revelations
The river of remorse
Bending from the vision
Unsteady in its course

River

of

Remorse

Wm Koch, Jr.   8-2-2014©

Slumber

An act of gentle and quiet
Water passing in a stream
With your comforting hug
Slumber teases with a dream
Of hours of days of despair
Care refuses to even heed
Minutes treasured solemn
Very little, all I really need
Sleep thus escapes me daily
Refuses to stay at all, at times
Weary from its night journey
In a mind, full of these rhymes
Welcomed in hopeless pleading
Not turning my back at all
Sad dreams burst the path taken
A nighttime of a constant fall
Marching and crying drown out
Ticking of a clock that rings
Encircled with agony's images
Harbinger of visions it brings
Past to the present struggles
Father with a sorrowful soul
Faced with memories so tough

Forever napping still my goal
An act of gentle and quiet
Water passing in a stream
With your comforting hug
Slumber teases with a dream

(6-23-2012)

Drop of Water

Drop of water with touch of class
Ventured across a pane of glass
Slowly gravitating to the ground
Moving gently without a sound
Like life itself, smooth and rough
Over diversions, easy or very tough
Journey long of a timeless travel
Fighting back to ageless unravel
Sunlit sparkles as a diamond cut
Soiled from dirt of a muddy rut
Raindrop, your trekking has no end
Gather with others your type, to spend
Each day and night in tragic search
Underfoot or from advantage perch
You'll evaporate soon to see tomorrow
Or become a tear from too much sorrow
Flowing in mass toward the open sea
In a hidden puddle, a wet foot for me
Warm and welcomed in summertime
Cold and biting, lost in winter rhyme
Sailing faster from winds of storms
Frozen on lakes as strange icy forms
Pattered on roofs with constant sounds

Christening graves at hallowed grounds
Holy water for last rites of the mass
Drop of water, with touch of class

(6-6-2012)

Sorrow Stands

Sad sorrow, like death
Waiting with pale concern
Always watching, always ready
Content to wait its own turn

Escape to another world
Sleep as you might try
Running forever in dreams
Visions in a silent cry

Life goes on, in time
Waits for no one at all
Wearing to the very last
Each rising sun shall fall

Dark brings visions of calm
Sorrow stands at your bed
Outlasts each nightmare
That dances in your head

Wavering not one bit
As sorrow never sleeps
Welcomes you in the morning
Your welfare he always keeps

Time passes each life
Death has his dates
Alas sweet sorrow follows
Even through, golden gates

(6-1-2013)

Sad sorrow, like death
Waiting with pale concern
Always watching, always ready
Content to wait its own turn
Escape to another world
Sleep as you might try
Running forever in dreams
Visions in a silent cry

Life goes on , in time
Waits for no one at all
Wearing to the very last
Each rising sun shall fall
Dark brings visions of calm
Sorrow stands at your bed
Outlasts each nightmare
That dances in your head

Wavering not one bit
As sorrow never sleeps
Welcomes you in the morning
Your welfare he always keeps
Time passes each life
Death has his dates
Alas sweet sorrow follows
Even through, golden gates

Sorrow Stands

Wm Koch Jr.   6-1-2013©

Sullen Eyes

Standing against the wind
In rain from summer skies
Where a heat dries a path
Memories pour sullen eyes

In a race to the very end
Conscience leads the way
Mind and body follow suit
Lonely night to lonesome day

Aching is the soul of heart
As is the heart of any soul
Pursuit of recall, paramount
Just like every living goal

Each emotion runs the course
Pointed elbow jabs the test
Chasing the past with spirits
Never giving the eternal rest

Running against the wind
Into air of timeless cries
As cold overtakes a trail
Daily steps of honest lies

Cover up the uncovered
Pretend to play the part
Feelings leave the trace
In passion, scorned rampart

Memories brings the dream
Ever longing with hopeless sighs
Which others can't understand
Belonging only to sullen eyes

(6-8-2014)

Sullen Eyes

Standing against the wind
In rain from summer skies
Where a heat dries a path
Memories pour sullen eyes

In a race to the very end
Conscience leads the way
Mind and body follow suit
Lonely night to lonesome day

Aching is the soul of heart
As is the heart of any soul
Pursuit of recall, paramount
Just like every living goal

Each emotion runs the course
Pointed elbow jabs the test
Chasing the past with spirits
Never giving the eternal rest

Running against the wind
Into air of timeless cries
As cold overtakes a trail
Daily steps of honest lies

Cover up the uncovered
Pretend to play the part
Feelings leave the trace
In passion, scorned rampart

Memories brings the dream
Ever longing with hopeless sighs
Which others can't understand
Belonging only to sullen eyes

Wm Koch Jr.
6-8-2014©

Valor

VALOR

val·ornoun \ˈva-lər\
: Courage or bravery

Full Definition of Valor

: Strength of mind or spirit that enables a person to encounter danger with firmness: personal bravery

Examples of Valor

- The soldiers received the nation's highest award for *valor*.

- <the absence of indecision even in the face of death is the true mark of *valor*>

Origin of Valor

Middle English valour worth, worthiness, bravery, from Anglo-French, from Medieval Latin valor, from Latin valēre to be of worth, be strong—more at wield
First Known Use: 14th century

Related to Valor

Synonyms

bottle [British slang], bravery, courageousness, daring, daringness, dauntlessness, doughtiness, fearlessness, gallantry, greatheartedness, guts, gutsiness, hardihood, heart, heroism, intestinal fortitude, intrepidity, intrepidness, moxie, nerve, pecker [chiefly British], prowess, stoutness, courage, virtue

Bold Colors

Freedom has a color
Its red or white or blue
Gold and purple majestic
These colors are also true
Paint a portrait of America
For freedom I shall fight
Protect those defenseless
Carry lady liberty's light
It's ingrain in our souls
That free men shall exist
Battle against tyranny
Wherever it shall persist
It's said for generations
Every day under the sun
Blue field with red and white
Bold colors that do not run
Heart of purple of the brave
Gold star for those that fall
Red and white are waving
Blue of the service call
These colors are so true
Of sacrifices and valor
Tribute and honor always
Freedom has a color

(6-9-2012)

Old Man Tree

Tree
Old man tree
Spread upward to the skies
Hopeful
Hopeful for an answer
To agony's constant cries
Rooted
Rooted in hallow soil
Standard bearer to the end
Sacrifice
Sacrifice of the brave
The courage that will defend
Guard
Guard of the future
That shall learn from the old
Uniform
Uniform of the proud
Reverence the colors blue to gold
Blossom
Blossom of the flowers
Draped on a tomb of the free
Seasons
Seasons for every time
The old man in the tree

(4-19-2013)

William Koch Jr.

Tree
Old man tree
Spread upward to the skies
Hopeful
Hopeful for an answer
To agony's constant cries
Rooted
Rooted in hallow soil
Standard bearer to the end
Sacrifice
Sacrifice of the brave
The courage that will defend
Guard
Guard of the future
That shall learn from the old
Uniform
Uniform of the proud
Reverence the colors blue to gold
Blossom
Blossom of the flowers
Draped on a tomb of the free
Seasons
Seasons for every time
The old man in the tree

Reach Across

Reach across
A hand, right there
Be not afraid
Nothing to fear

Rise to a resting
Dreams go to die
Happy it's not
Forever shall cry

Into the clouds
As sun disappears
Angels go toting
Pails of your tears

Spirits survive
As only they will
In memories now
Just over the hill

A shadow of dark
Casts a heavy heart
Souls of sorrow
Of loving depart

William Koch Jr.

Fear is alone
Afraid of the loss
Right there, a hand
Reach across

(5-14-2012)

Four Leaf Clovers

Whispering dreams, disappear
Like love songs that are over
Lost melodies concerning care
I seek my own four leaf clover

Flowers that have Lord's faith above
With eternal hope on one leaf arm
Aligned with the petal of love
A fourth reveals a lucky charm
In fields of pleasant of thought
Covered in clubs of the trinity
Shamrocks of blessing are sought
As my search turns old for me

Gentle breeze warms the heart
Meadows of golden grass below
Quest that ended at the very start
How life now passes ever so slow
Dreams that whisper as they tear
On a stripe of honor called Dover
A tragic answer to all I did fear
Now missing, my four leaf clover

(4-9-2012)

A Bravest Son

Meant to be for any son or daughter
Follow me
On a path
Behind a soul
Of a son

Fresh of face
Toughest beard
Chute packed
Toting a gun

Radio ready
Gunner helm
Soco journey
Shots for fun

Ice cold food
Too hot days
Dark of moon
Light by sun

Shoulder to shoulder
Bond of blood
Arms in brothers
Band on the run

Courage strong
Spirit step
Dedication heart
Missed a ton

Send me
On a path
To follow
A bravest son

(5-11-2013)

A Bravest Son

Follow me
On a path
Behind a soul
Of a son

Fresh of face
Toughest beard
Chute packed
Toting a gun
Radio ready
Gunner helm
Soco journey
Shots for fun

Ice cold food
Too hot days
Dark of moon
Light by sun

Shoulder to shoulder
Bond of blood
Arms in brothers
Band on the run
Courage strong
Spirit step
Dedication heart
Missed a ton

Send me
On a path
To follow
A bravest son

Wm Koch Jr.   3-11-2013©

All and the Any

I sit here all alone
Alone with sorrow write
Penning words of dreams
Dreams beyond daylight
With thoughts of the few
Too few to the mass many
Longing from a journey
Journey, all and the any
There's the all, as everyone
Everyone on their course
With the any are the scarce
Scarce born from a source
Masses being the blind
Blind from a reality
Few with the vision
Vision to really see
Groups of numbers hide
Hide clearly in the sun
As a scant lies in the wait
Waiting on the run

Daily goes by a path
A path of day and night
The route never taken
Taken on the plight
All and the any

Any, walk the line
Protected are the all
All, remain just fine
Land is the home
Home of the brave
Heart or soul courage
Courage, freedom gave

There's the all, as everyone
Everyone on their course
With the any are the scarce
Scarce born from a source

(7-15-2014)

I sit here all alone
Alone with sorrow write
Penning words of dreams
Dreams beyond daylight
With thoughts of the few
Too few to the mass many
Longing from a journey
Journey, all and the any
There's the all, as everyone
Everyone on their course
With the any are the scarce
Scarce born from a source
Masses being the blind
Blind from a reality
Few with the vision
Vision to really see
Groups of numbers hide
Hide clearly in the sun
As a scant lies in the wait
Waiting on the run

Daily goes by a path
A path of day and night
The route never taken
Taken on the plight
All and the any
Any, walk the line
Protected are the all
All, remain just fine
Land is the home
Home of the brave
Heart or soul courage
Courage, freedom gave

There's the all, as everyone
Everyone on their course
With the any are the scarce
Scarce born from a source

All and the Any

Wm Koch Jr.
7-15-2014©

The Price

They train and fight, they pay the price
Tribute their service, salute their sacrifice
Where courage to serve is a nation's call
Coming from the heart, one standing tall

From across the country, young and the old
The plains to the rockies, mountains of gold
City street or farm road will lead the way
Shores of oceans, towns of each harbor bay

Marching to the cadence of the Army bound
Marine landing, Air Force above the ground
At sea with guardsmen or aboard a naval ship
Branches that defend from each base to the tip

Spanning the world from these United States
Protecting freedom, carrying liberty's weights
Of justice and rights, that made America great
Religious freedom on a constitutional plate

Founders foretold of rough seas ahead
Of battles and wars, blood spilling red
Freedom is not free, that is all too clear
Yet, courage to defend is all the brave hear

Standing tall with courage of the heart
A nation's call, your love one must part
Tribute their service, salute their sacrifice
They train and fight, they pay the price

(9-19-2012)

Soco Soldiers

Soco soldiers
Count one by one
Fighting ready
Gear, chute and gun
Out of Bragg
Double A in tow
Soco shots down
Ready to go
On call to arms
Protecting the land
Hour by hour
Mountains and sand
Drop zone power
Fury from the sky
Toast to praise
To do or to die
Nation secured
Boots on the ground
Shots are taken
Round by round
Victory is ours
Call of duty loud
Standing strong
History is proud
Battles are won

High and low
Tributes and honors
Soldiers of Soco

(7-26-2012)

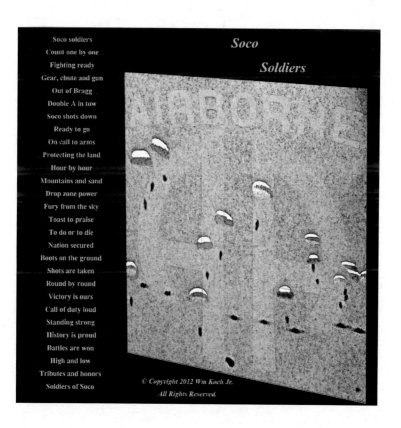

Ageless Warriors

Ageless warriors
Thru dark or light
Courage flows swift
To carry the fight
Of brave souls alive
Carry hearts of gold
Battle of the rages
Bygone tales are told
Cast in dedication
Walk of the line
Strength to resist
Thoughts of mine
Protect the fragile
Defend the weak
Encounter injustice
Liberty they seek
Venture to the era
Clash in the end
Knights of the ages
Days to suspend
Draped in ever sorrow
Redemption confess
To carry the fight
Warriors now, ageless

(5-12-2013)

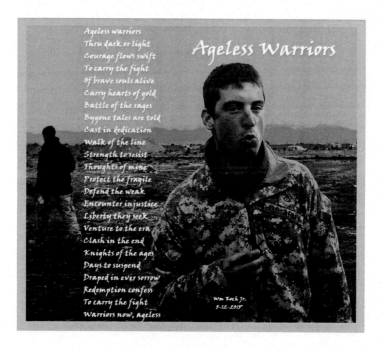

Ageless warriors
Thru dark or light
Courage flows swift
To carry the fight
Of brave souls alive
Carry hearts of gold
Battle of the rages
Bygone tales are told
Cast in dedication
Walk of the line
Strength to resist
Thoughts of mine
Protect the fragile
Defend the weak
Encounter injustice
Liberty they seek
Venture to the era
Clash in the end
Knights of the ages
Days to suspend
Draped in ever sorrow
Redemption confess
To carry the fight
Warriors now, ageless

Ageless Warriors

Wm Koch Jr.
5-12-2015

Can't Go Back

I've got emotion, the dream I lack
I'm going home now, I can't go back
Mind on my soldiers, ablaze and afire
Pressing forward as things were dire
Not taking bets on the red or the black
This is combat fears, no jokers, no jack
Home soil of the brave and of the strong
You know the one, the American song

Liberty and justice, freedom of rights
Of fighting the enemy in many a fights
Defending others, a job that's a cause
Protect those golden rules and laws
Not calling you out or having some fun
We're talking living at the end of a gun
Stand for the eagle, bearing your claws
Helping brothers, get though each pause

Battle wounds are not always seen
Fatigue of the mind, a fanatical fiend
Defending others, of the toll it takes
Protecting liberty at the highest stakes
This is war and we fought the good fight
Turn to shadows at home in the night
Never the same as it was ever before
That part of our life has exit the door

We'll march again and fill the need
Battle worn torn and ready to bleed
Homeward bound and flag as a drape
Medals of honors are the tale of the tape
Marching to a song that begs us to save
A great nation as the home of the brave
Freedom calls us, we answer it loud
We're Americans dam it, we wear it proud

Mind on my soldiers, ablaze and afire
Pressing forward as things were dire
I've got emotion, the dream I lack
I'm going home now, I can't go back

(Summer 2012, 7-5-2013)

Can't Go Back   Wm Koch Jr   Summer 2012 / 7-3-2013

I've got emotion, the dream I lack
I'm going home now, I can't go back
Mind on my soldiers, ablaze and afire
Pressing forward as things were dire

Not taking bets on the red or the black
This is combat fears, no jokers, no jack
Home soil of the brave and of the strong
You know the one, the American song

Liberty and justice, freedom of rights
Of fighting the enemy in many a fights
Defending others, a job that's a cause
Protect those golden rules and laws

Not calling you out or having some fun
We're talking living at the end of a gun
Stand for the eagle, bearing your claws
Helping brothers, get though each pause

Battle wounds are not always seen
Fatigue of the mind, a fanatical fiend
Defending others, of the toll it takes
Protecting liberty at the highest stakes

This is war and we fought the good fight
Turn to shadows at home in the night
Never the same as it was ever before
That part of our life has exit the door

We'll march again and fill the need
Battle worn torn and ready to bleed
Homeward bound and flag as a drape
Medals of honors are the tale of the tape

Marching to a song that begs us to save
A great nation as the home of the brave
Freedom calls us, we answer it loud
We're Americans dam it, we wear it proud

Mind on my soldiers, ablaze and afire
Pressing forward as things were dire
I've got emotion, the dream I lack
I'm going home now, I can't go back

Oh Conscience

My thoughts crushed, sad and full of tears
I reach for you, across the lonely years
In you are my hopes, to see me through
Join with me now and forever, forever true
What seemed a yesterday, it's been so long
Being too weak, you've kept me very strong
Losing what we had, there's no going back
Can you rebuild with me, what we now lack
A lasting tie with trusting, a life on the run
Day or night in moonlight, or a rising sun
Oh conscience, you're away much too much
I've lost myself, to the meaningless touch
Free to make mistakes, as we always do
Sharing the blame, along a guilty avenue
Lead me to the knowledge, to understand
Take me on a path, by the helping hand
There's no course set, or map to follow
Hills and spills, with dashed hopes hollow
Oh conscience, don't look away from me
As the mirror of the mind, is all you'll see
What seemed a yesterday, it's been so long
Being too weak, you've kept me very strong
In reaching for you, a comfort that nears
Oh conscience, still sad and full of tears

(12-26-2013)

Conclusion

More words and images will spill from the thoughts, dreams, and nightmares that shall continue on this journey. There's no closure, no healing, and little reconciliation of a broken heart and sorrowful soul.

That is just how it is, resigned to the path, trying to be prepared for the rest of the walk, crowded but still alone.

I would hope that you found some emotion or reflection in the preceding poems and verses that you can use in your own life and possibility give you a slight more compassion or caring. Those traits are sorely missing in much of the world today, and there can never be enough salutes to those that serve our nation in the Armed Forces, those organizations and groups that support them and our veterans. Tribute to those wounded by war or lost in the battle can never spell the whole story or the glory, these words try in vain at times; try to bring their sacrifice to the forefront of the nation and communities of the country where they belong.

I close this short meeting of ours with my thanks and appreciation for taking some time to read and feel the words along with a sense to the images that come from the deepest parts of a soul torn by loss, strife and a spiritual ordeal.

Sometimes, just sometimes…dragging the past
through the present is the only future.

—William Koch Jr.

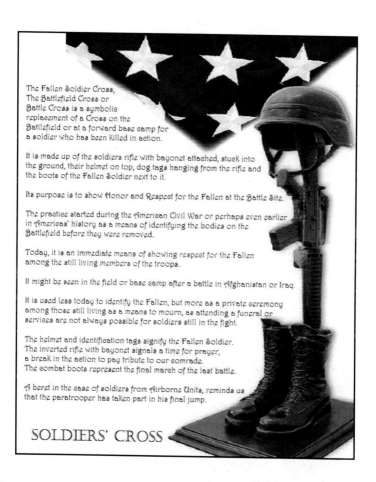

The Fallen Soldier Cross,
The Battlefield Cross or
Battle Cross is a symbolic
replacement of a Cross on the
Battlefield or at a forward base camp for
a soldier who has been killed in action.

It is made up of the soldiers rifle with bayonet attached, stuck into
the ground, their helmet on top, dog tags hanging from the rifle and
the boots of the Fallen Soldier next to it.

Its purpose is to show Honor and Respect for the Fallen at the Battle Site.

The practice started during the American Civil War or perhaps even earlier
in Americas' history as a means of identifying the bodies on the
Battlefield before they were removed.

Today, it is an immediate means of showing respect for the Fallen
among the still living members of the troops.

It might be seen in the field or base camp after a battle in Afghanistan or Iraq.

It is used less today to identify the Fallen, but more as a private ceremony
among those still living as a means to mourn, as attending a funeral or
services are not always possible for soldiers still in the fight.

The helmet and identification tags signify the Fallen Soldier.
The inverted rifle with bayonet signals a time for prayer,
a break in the action to pay tribute to our comrade.
The combat boots represent the final march of the last battle.

A beret in the case of soldiers from Airborne Units, reminds us
that the paratrooper has taken part in his final jump.

SOLDIERS' CROSS

EMCOR Corporation Diamond Award
Acceptance Speech

April 1, 2013

In being chosen for the Diamond Award from EMCOR, my thoughts are of reflecting on the people and groups that made this honor possible and the attributes that go into an award of this importance. For those making it possible and an organization like EMCOR, I thank President and CEO Mr. Tony Guzzi and his staff that went through the review of presentations and that selection process. I learned after hearing of their selection that there are many deserving of such an honor in the EMCOR family and the Diamond Award is a very humbling event for me, and just to be considered is a great honor. To EMCOR Company; Forest Electric of New Jersey, President Harry Sassaman and the staff here that put together the presentation for EMCOR to review. It was very gracious of them to have the thoughtfulness and concern to think that I would be worthy of the honor and to have it be presented by them is very special. I also thank them for their efforts of putting all this together today for the ceremony. To coworkers, friends, families, and organizations that have also been part of the times, trials, tribulations and distress of a blue collar, middle class family from New Jersey, I thank you all for your support, patience, concern and thoughts.

Continued reflection goes to my parents, William Sr. and Marion. Both have passed on from our daily lives but their service to our country during WWII and the faithful influence on my family and I are still impacting us today. Their guidance and caring attributes were the building blocks of my life and I found myself dedicated to try and pass those same attributes on to my family.

With heartfelt reflection is of my family that includes my wife Christine, our children Lynne, Bill and Steven. We are just one family of many, with patriotic passion, pride in service to others and respect for those that represent "Honor Above All." Without them and their love and concern for each other and me, none of this is possible or even conceivable.

A Koch family dedicated to each other with courage to help others while trying to do what is right. A faith in the guidance of a higher power in Jesus Christ, along with compassion for each other and concern for others welfare. A family, much like any other in America that participated in sports or activities like baseball and basketball for Bill and Steven with cheering leading and softball for Lynne. Of Jersey shore vacations that Christine would take the kids on each summer to Wildwood or Manasquan beaches here in New Jersey. Day trips to the Point Pleasant, Seaside Park, or local lakes. There were horseback riding, skateboarding, going to school, camps and onto colleges and the armed services for Steven with some growing pains along the way.

William Koch Jr.

Of a weathered resolve in work, school, and play through church or community service and local events. An average family that went to parades and fireworks on the Fourth of July, volunteered at church and school events or attended ball games together. In reflection, just a normal family in America that is transformed into a family of a Gold Star Fallen Hero in Cpl. Steven R. Koch, with the added anguish of losing a fallen angel in Lynne Koch. One member of this family Steven; volunteered to defend a line. Another member of this family Lynne; crossed over a different type of line. Christine, Bill, and I find ourselves standing at both of these lines every hour of every day. We have no choice but to continue on a path with dedication, courage, faith and compassion.

In that short retrospect, I accept the EMCOR Award for 2012 as a representative of my family of five with sincere honor and humility.

In that, this family of five has now grown again to be supported by EMCOR and Forest Electric to tribute and honor those individuals and groups that illustrate the attributes of dedication, courage, faith, and compassion with a tested resolve and a spiritual reflection.

The same dedication and courage set forth by a son and brother, Cpl. Steven R. Koch, Eighty-Second Airborne, KIA on March 3, 2008 in Afghanistan.

A faith and compassion shown by a daughter and sister, Lynne C. Koch, who left us on May 6, 2010, from post-traumatic stress disorder, from the loss of her brother, Steven.

EMCOR and Forest Electric with dedication and courage expressed the same faith and compassion to my family and to others on these lines of defense and struggle of sorrow with this honor here today.

EMCOR and Forest Electric reveal their resolve and reflection to core values of a concern to a family, to dedication to others and also to freedom. These values, now anguished and emotional in our Koch family, yet shared in the same resolve and reflection by Christine, young Bill and I. These emotions and traits are what continue to carry the remaining three of us to tribute and honor not only Steven and Lynne, but to those that serve the nation in the Armed Forces. To help those that care for the warriors or family members that are suffering the wounds of war, whether those wounds are physical, mental, emotional, or spiritual. This tribute and honor also extends in our efforts to aid veteran, charity and faith based groups that support the troops, veterans and wounded warriors.

We focus on the dedication and courage of groups like the Eighty-Second Airborne Infantry; Steven's Army family, the American Legion Post 25 of Milltown with their continual help to our family and all veterans and troops, the Army ROTC of New Jersey's State University of Rutgers, for their direct service to the nation and their honor to Cpl. Steven R. Koch in their annual Warriors Run. A run to raise funds and awareness for wounded warriors in partnership with an amazing organization, Hope for the Warriors.

In faith and compassion, we lean on the Our Lady of Lourdes parish family of Milltown, NJ for our beliefs and guidance, in the Hope for the Warriors organization for their support to the troops, veterans and families with wounds that are seen and unseen. To the International Brotherhood of Electrical Workers Local 456 of New Brunswick, New Jersey, which has been a large part of our Koch family for generations and with their great support to our family with the loss of both Steven and Lynne.

I, myself, personally try to extend those traits of dedication, courage, faith and compassion through books of written verses, images and expressions of emotion through Tate Publishing. Emotions felt by all of us going through the tested resolve and reflection of the sacrifice of soldiers and the pain of losing family members too soon.

We, as a family, resolve to carry the baton of Cpl. Steven R. Koch in his dedication and courage to defend his family, freedom and America along with protecting those that cannot protect themselves. That last part was the most important to Steven. Protecting others that were defenseless! In his volunteering for service, we four and now three have been drafted to continue in any way possible. We salute Cpl. Steven Koch, all the troops and all those Fallen Heroes in the defense of freedom.

We reflect in the knowledge to carry that faith and compassion of a young woman who loved too much. In losing her battle to Post Traumatic Stress Disorder, Lynne also became a casualty of war. In her heart she lost a brother, a soldier, a best friend and in our family she was like a "little mother," she felt she lost a son.

These organizations and groups with the people that belong to each of them that I mentioned have all helped Christine, Bill, and I through this path we now walk. A pathway that now has the support of EMCOR and Forest Electric. With such a prestigious corporation honor, the EMCOR Diamond Award, it serves in that same resolve and reflection to continue to honor those that dedicate their lives and have courage to defend America, freedom and those that cannot protect themselves. With faith and compassion, EMCOR and Forest Electric stand with us in the support and tribute to those that defend our nation, wounded warriors and family. I thank EMCOR and Forest Electric with sincere gratitude for this honor and the opportunity to express those emotions and expressions of the entire Koch family, here today.

In closing and with much appreciation in humble reverence for this award, I leave two quotes for all of you to consider. One is of resolve to continue with whatever courage you have left even when your dedication is weak from sorrow or distress, "Don't question where courage comes from; be hopeful it never runs out." The other is in reflection toward a faith and the compassion to carry on a path of dedication that sums up one of my feelings toward Cpl. Steven R. Koch, "The footprint of a hero leaves an everlasting path to follow."

Thank you all very much.